YOUR KNOWLEDGE HAS VALUE

Bibliographic information published by the German National Library:

The German National Library lists this publication in the National Bibliography; detailed bibliographic data are available on the Internet at http://dnb.dnb.de .

Imprint:

Copyright © 2018 GRIN Verlag
Print and binding: Books on Demand GmbH, Norderstedt Germany
ISBN: 9783346052414

This book at GRIN:

https://www.grin.com/document/502807

Max Schmidt

What explains cross-national variation in efforts to address climate change?

GRIN Verlag

GRIN - Your knowledge has value

Since its foundation in 1998, GRIN has specialized in publishing academic texts by students, college teachers and other academics as e-book and printed book. The website www.grin.com is an ideal platform for presenting term papers, final papers, scientific essays, dissertations and specialist books.

Visit us on the internet:

http://www.grin.com/

http://www.facebook.com/grincom

http://www.twitter.com/grin_com

What explains cross-national variation in efforts to address climate change?

Contents

1. Introduction

This essay will analyse one possible cause for addressing climate change with varying efforts that is often neglected in the climate policy literature: countries' vulnerability to climate-related risks (e.g. floods, droughts, tropical storms). Under the most important factors that influence the degree to which a country is vulnerable are its geographical location and level of economic development. Hence, exacerbated by their dependency on especially vulnerable economic sectors such as agriculture, low income countries face the biggest climate-related risks (Kreft et al. 2017).

Generally, two ways of addressing climate change can be differentiated: *adaptation* and *mitigation*. While most of the adaptation literature to the minimization of climate-related risks is about strategies of developing countries, literature about their mitigation efforts – understood here as policy decisions to reduce greenhouse gas (GHG) emissions – is still rare. A similar picture can be drawn for emerging economies – countries that are not recognised as industrialised countries, despite the high growth rates of their Gross Domestic Product (GDP) and newly emerging middle classes (Khanna and Palepu 2010). Thus, the question can be raised to what extent vulnerability is a reason for them to address climate change.

To explore this topic, I will firstly lay out a research design (Most Similar Systems) that enables us to compare the vulnerability and mitigation efforts of Brazil, India and South Africa. I will focus on these countries and their mitigation efforts since they are among the biggest emerging economies which are, in general, expected to be "*by far the most important source of future emission growth*" (Urpelainen and van de Graaf 2017: 6). Based on my findings in the subsequent analysis, it can be said that a country's vulnerability to climate-related risks plays

1

no significant role for mitigating GHG emissions and consequently addressing climate change. This main argument will be critically discussed in the conclusion and research gaps identified.

2. Research design

In this essay, the dependent variable will be the strength of mitigation efforts of Brazil, India and South Africa to reduce their GHG emissions. As one of the two components of climate policy, the strength of mitigation efforts can be understood as the *"extent to which the statutory provisions of climate policies are likely to restrict GHG emissions if implemented as intended"* (Compston and Bailey 2016: 145). Suitable indicators to measure this extent are *policy outputs* (levels of political commitment to mitigation) and *policy outcomes* (emission levels and trends) (Bättig and Bernauer 2009: 281). These indicators will be compared by drawing to country's Intended Nationally Determined Contributions (INDC's), the trajectory of their GHG emissions, and an index measuring their climate change performance.

The independent variable, a country's vulnerability to climate-related risks, can be defined as *"the degree to which a system is susceptible to, and unable to cope with, adverse effects of climate change, including climate variability and extremes [...]"* (International Panel on Climate Change 2007). This variable will be operationalized by assessing the three countries' self-perceived degree of concern and another index measuring their experience with climate-related risks. Hence, the following hypothesis can be derived:

The higher a country's vulnerability to climate-related risks, the stronger are its efforts to mitigate GHG emissions, and vice versa.

This hypothesis will be tested with three emerging economies (Brazil, India and South Africa) since they fulfil many criteria of a valid Most Similar Systems Design. Other emerging economies such as Mexico or China could not be considered, mainly because of limited space but also due to deviations such as their regime types (The Economist Intelligence Unit 2017). The three chosen countries do not only achieve similar results in rankings to the state of their democracy (Ibid.: 6) and are repeatedly listed under the world's biggest GHG emitters (Olivier et al. 2017), they are also frequently classified as large middle-income countries which have experienced increasing pressure to shoulder their own part of the mitigation burden (e.g. Jaeger and Michaelowa 2016: 940; Michaelowa and Michaelowa 2012).

3. Analysis

A first indicator measuring the three countries' varying degrees of vulnerability to climate-related risks is their self-assessment as illustrated in *Table 1*.[1]

Table 1

Country	Description of own vulnerability	Most vulnerable areas	Internal rank of vulnerability
Brazil	Stresses need to protect vulnerable populations and communities	/	3
India	Highlights that few countries are as vulnerable as it; 85% of areas vulnerable to one or multiple hazards	Agrarian economy, expansive coastal areas, Himalayan region and islands; differs among states, regions (also within) and groups	1
South Africa	Perceives itself as particularly vulnerable	Water and food security, health, human settlements, infrastructure and ecosystem services	2

Sources: United Nations Framework Convention on Climate Change (UNFCCC) 2015a, UNFCCC 2015b, UNFCCC 2015c; own illustration

In quantifying countries' vulnerability to climate-related risks, the Climate Risk Index (CRI) is frequently used. The CRI, compiled by the think tank Germanwatch, considers the indicators a) absolute number of deaths, b) number of deaths per 100.000 inhabitants, c) sum of losses in US$ in purchasing power parity and d) losses per unit of GDP (Kreft et al. 2017).

---

[1] The author is aware that this only represents a subjective assessment. Nevertheless, a qualitative analysis may come to a similar ranking.

Table 2

Country	CRI Rank 1996-2015	CRI Rank 2013	CRI Rank 2014	CRI Rank 2015	CRI Rank average 2013-2015 (rounded)*	Internal Rank
Brazil	89	78	21	87	62	3
India	14	17	10	4	10	1
South Africa	89	74	37	33	48	2

*based on own calculations

Sources: Kreft et al. 2017, Kreft et al. 2016, Kreft et al. 2015; own illustration

Drawing on the CRI, it becomes clear that the three emerging economies show different degrees of vulnerability to climate-related risks (*Table 2*). The internal ranking is identical with the one in *Table 1*, for both the current CRI Rank and the average of the years 2013-2015. This finding validates that India is the most vulnerable country, followed by South Africa and then Brazil. Both for India and South Africa a trend can be surmised that these countries will be more vulnerable to climate-related risks in the future. This thesis, however, must not be seen as empirically valid but rather as one possible trend among others since the CRI is based on past data and is explicitly not designed for linear protections of future climate impacts (Kreft et al. 2017: 3).

Having briefly assessed to which degree the three states are vulnerable, in the next step light must be shed on their self-imposed Intended Nationally Determined Contributions as a form of policy-output. INDC's are short and longer-term national targets to reduce GHG emissions, adopted by the responsible Conference of the Parties (COP) with a view to COP 21 in Paris in 2015.

Table 3

Country	Timeframe	INDC – reduction targets, base year: 2005	Target type of emission mitigation
Brazil	2025	37%	absolute
	2030	43% (indicative)	absolute
	2025	66%	emission intensity of GDP*
	2030	75%	emission intensity of GDP
India	2030	33-35%	emission intensity of GDP
South Africa	2020-2025	reach peak	absolute
	2025-2035	stabilize emission level	absolute
	2035 onwards	permanent reduction	absolute

*= t CO_2e/GDP (1000 US$)

Sources: UNFCCC 2015a, UNFCCC 2015b, UNFCCC 2015c, Damassa et al. 2015; own illustration

Between Brazil, India and South Africa, as contrasting data in *Table 3* illustrates, they vary significantly. Clearly opposing the hypothesis, India as most vulnerable state is not undertaking the strongest efforts to limit its GHG emissions. Furthermore, Brazil as the least vulnerable country has set itself the highest ambitions whereas South Africa shows nearly no efforts at all. Their comparability, however, must be limited due to different target types, timeframes and current level of GHG emissions per capita (Burck et al. 2017). Moreover, these numbers represent the first internationally binding mitigation targets of the three emerging economies since they, in contrast to industrialized countries, had no formal obligations under the predecessor of the Paris Agreement (Kyoto Protocol, 2008-2020).

Figure 1: Five-year trend ([%], 2011-2016) in CO₂ emissions versus non-CO₂ emissions per country / region for G20 countries

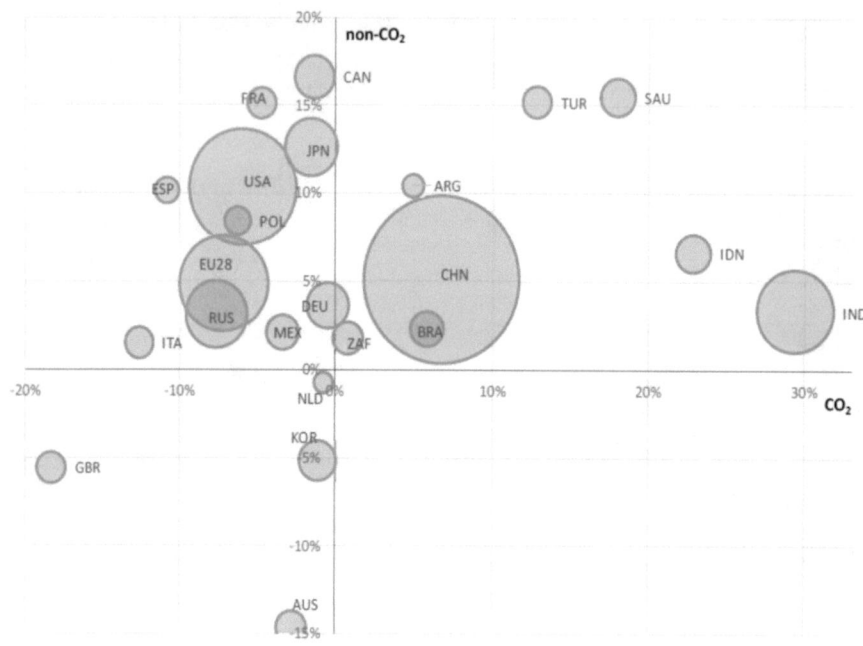

Consequently, their GHG emissions increased steadily over the last few years, as illustrated in *Figure 1* (Olivier et al. 2017: 12). This trajectory, in turn, made it more difficult to set themselves ambitious targets for the time after 2020 when the Paris Agreement enters into force. To the same time, some scholars highlight that although India's absolute emissions increased significantly over the last few years (now it belongs to the ten largest CO_2-emitting countries), its per capita emissions are still relatively low (Burck et al. 2017: 4).

Another commonly used index to measure countries' mitigation efforts is Germanwatch's Climate Change Performance Index (CCPI), a ranking of the 58 countries that are responsible for 90% of the global GHG emissions. Based on the components emission level (weighting 30%), development of emissions (30%), renewable energies (10%), efficiency (10%) and climate policy (20%) (Burck et al. 2017: 9), India is listed before Brazil (rank 40) and South Africa (32) on rank 20 (Ibid.: 12 f.) – a result in accordance with the hypothesis.

The explanatory power of the CCPI, however, must be limited since the measurement of the indicators is based on a single year. In 2016, for example, India achieved nearly the same ranking (23) while South Africa (48) was ranked behind Brazil (42) (Ibid.). For 2015, however, a similar picture to the one in 2017 can be drawn (Burck et al. 2016) that speaks against the validity of the hypothesis.

The only small N-study known to the author that include the three emerging economies in its exploration of the relation between my independent and dependent variable draws the clear conclusion that vulnerability plays no significant role for explaining mitigation efforts (Rong 2010). Although Rong (2010: 4589) uses the common definition of 'vulnerability' from the IPCC – the very same I use – she ascribes Brazil (medium), India (high) and South Africa (low) different vulnerabilities from those that the CRI and I do. This may be due to her reliance on older data and the fact that she considers their mitigation capability as a separate category, which limits the comparability with the other findings presented here.

4. Conclusion

In this essay, I have questioned as to whether the vulnerability of a country to climate-related risks can explain the strength of its mitigation efforts. Comparing the three emerging economies Brazil, India and South Africa, I draw the conclusion that a country's vulnerability plays no significant role for the strength of mitigation efforts and therewith to address climate change. It remains an open question to what extent this finding can be generalized because industrialised and developing countries can not only be assumed to have varying degrees of vulnerability but also different capabilities to mitigate GHG emissions. The same is true for other emerging economies since this category include countries from nearly every world region – characterised by diverse geographical conditions. The influence of per capita GHG emission-targets on the strength of mitigation efforts remains an open question, too. South Africa, however, does not mention them at all in its INDC's, and therefore a comparison regarding them could not be conducted in this essay.

Against the background that both India (UNFCCC 2015b) and South Africa (UNFCCC 2015c) clearly state their expected increasing vulnerability, the question can be raised if a country's vulnerability could not play a more important role in the future. This is especially important to note considering that some authors (e.g. Never and Betz 2014: 3) argue that vulnerability is not among the decisive factors for environmental performance – a strong argument based only on Rong's (2010) study – and hence completely neglect it for replication studies. Moreover, since I focused on the well-measured empirical vulnerability, more research should be done about

7

the correlation between public awareness of vulnerability and addressing climate change, as Michaelowa and Michaelowa (2012) exemplify with India's changed role in international climate negotiations, and different dimensions of vulnerability (Buys et al. 2009). Only by closing these research gaps can vulnerability be explored further as a possible factor contributing to a countries' mitigation efforts.

Bibliography

Bättig, M.B. and Bernauer, T. 2009, 'National Institutions and Global Public Goods: Are Democracies More Cooperative in Climate Change Policy?', *International Organization*, vol. 63, no. 2, pp. 281-308.

Burck, J., Marten, F. and Bals, C. 2016, *The Climate Change Performance Index – Results 2016*, Bonn, Berlin and Brussels: Germanwatch and Climate Action Network Europe.

Burck, J., Marten, F. and Bals, C. 2017, *Climate Change Performance Index – Results 2017*, Bonn, Berlin and Brussels: Germanwatch and Climate Action Network Europe.

Buys, P., Deichmann, U., Meisner, C., Ton That, T. and Wheeler, D. 2009, 'Country stakes in climate change negotiations: two dimensions of vulnerability', *Climate Policy*, vol. 9, no. 3, pp. 288-305.

Compston, H. and Bailey, I. 2016, 'Climate Policy strength compared: China, the US, the EU, India, Russia and Japan', *Climate Policy*, vol. 16, no. 2, pp. 145-164.

Damassa, T., Fransen, T., Haya, B., Ge, M., Pjeczka, K. and Ross, K. 2015, *Interpreting INDCs: Assessing Transparency of Post-2020 Greenhouse Gas Emissions Targets for 8 TOP-Emitting Economies*, Working Paper, Washington, DC: World Resources Institute.

International Panel on Climate Change 2007, *Working Group II: Impacts, Adaptation and Vulnerability – Glossary*, online, [Available:] https://www.ipcc.ch/publications_and_data/ar4/wg2/en/annexessglossary-e-o.html [2018, 2nd April].

Jaeger, M.D. and Michaelowa, K. 2016, 'Global climate policy and local energy politics: is India hiding behind the poor?', *Climate Policy*, vol. 16, no. 7, pp. 940-951.

Khanna, T. and Palepu, K.G. 2010, 'How To Define Emerging Markets', *Forbes*, online, [Available:] https://www.forbes.com/2010/05/27/winning-in-emerging-markets-opinions-book-excerpts-khanna-palepu.html#3564e6a460c4 [2018, 2nd April].

Kreft, S., Eckstein, D., Junghans, L., Kerestan, C. and Hagen, U. 2015, *Global Climate Risk Index 2015 – Who Suffers Most From Extreme Weather Events? Weather-related Loss Events in 2013 and 1994 to 2013*, Briefing Paper, Bonn: Germanwatch.

Kreft, S., Eckstein, D., Dorsch, L. and Fischer, L. 2016, *Global Climate Risk Index 2016 – Who Suffers Most From Extreme Weather Events? Weather-related Loss Events in 2014 and 1995 to 2014*, Briefing Paper, Bonn: Germanwatch.

Kreft, S., Eckstein, D. and Melchior, I. 2017, *Global Climate Risk Index 2017 – Who Suffers Most From Extreme Weather Events? Weather-related Loss Events in 2015 and 1996 to 2015*, Briefing Paper, Bonn: Germanwatch.

Michaelowa, K. and Michaelowa, A. 2012, 'India as an emerging power in international climate negotiations', *Climate Policy*, vol. 12, no. 5, pp. 575-590.

Never, B. and Betz, J. 2014, 'Comparing the Climate Policy Performance of Emerging Economies', *World Development*, vol. 59, no. 1, pp. 1-15.

Olivier, J.G.J., Schure, K.M. and Peters, J.A.H.W. 2017, *Trends in global CO$_2$ and total greenhouse gas emissions. 2017 Report*, The Hague: PBL Netherlands Environmental Assessment Agency, online, [Available:] http://www.pbl.nl/sites/default/files/cms/publicaties/pbl-2017-trends-in-global-co2-and-total-greenhouse-gas-emissons-2017-report_2674.pdf [2018, 2nd April].

Rong, F. 2010, 'Understanding developing country stances on post-2012 climate change negotiations: Comparative analysis of Brazil, China, India, Mexico and South Africa', *Energy Policy*, vol. 38, no. 8, pp. 4582-4591.

The Economist Intelligence Unit 2017, *Democracy Index 2017 – Free speech under attack*, online, [Available:] www.eiu.com/Handlers/WhitepaperHandler.ashx?fi=Democracy_Index_2017.pdf&mode=wp &campaignid=DemocracyIndex2017 [2018, 2nd April].

UNFCCC 2015, *Federative Republic of Brazil: Intended Nationally Determined Contribution towards achieving the objective of the United Nations Framework Convention on Climate Change*, online, [Available:] http://www4.unfccc.int/submissions/INDC/Published%20Documents/Brazil/1/BRAZIL%20i NDC%20english%20FINAL.pdf [2018, 2nd April].

UNFCCC 2015, *India's Intended Nationally Determined Contribution: Working Towards Climate Justice*, online, [Available:] http://www4.unfccc.int/submissions/INDC/Published%20Documents/India/1/INDIA%20IND C%20TO%20UNFCCC.pdf [2018, 2nd April].

UNFCCC 2015, *South Africa's Intended Nationally Determined Contribution (INDC)*, online, [Available:] http://www4.unfccc.int/submissions/INDC/Published%20Documents/India/1/INDIA http://www4.unfccc.int/submissions/INDC/Published%20Documents/South%20Africa/1/Sout h%20Africa.pdf [2018, 2nd April].

Urpelainen, J. and Van de Graaf, T. 2017, 'United States non-cooperation and the Paris agreement', *Climate Policy*, online, [Available:] https://www.tandfonline.com/doi/full/10.1080/14693062.2017.1406843 [2018, 2nd April].

YOUR KNOWLEDGE HAS VALUE

- We will publish your bachelor's and
  master's thesis, essays and papers

- Your own eBook and book -
  sold worldwide in all relevant shops

- Earn money with each sale

Upload your text at www.GRIN.com
and publish for free